The Adventu
Zara and the Kindness
Crystals

IAN BARRETT

ISBN: 9798398297959

DEDICATION

This book is dedicated to my wife Katherine, and my two children Isaac & Emily. May happiness fill your lives forever.

One sunny morning, in a universe far far away Zara ventured into the enchanted forest, her heart filled with curiosity and excitement. She stumbled upon sparkling crystals hidden among the mossy rocks and trees, its vibrant colours captivating her

As Zara picked up the crystal, a soft glow enveloped her, and a gentle voice whispered, "Kindness is the key." Intrigued, Zara gathered her friends, and they set off on a quest to discover the crystal's true power.

Zara's first stop was the meadow, where she encountered a group of playful bunnies. Zara shared her lunch with them, and the crystal shimmered with warmth, spreading kindness and joy.

In the enchanted forest, Zara met a mischievous squirrel who had lost its acorns. Together, she searched high and low, gathering acorns and returning them to the squirrel's cozy home. The crystal glowed brighter, radiating kindness to all.

Next, they stumbled upon a grumpy old owl perched high in a tree. Zara and her friends sang a cheerful song, bringing smiles to the owl's face. The crystal glimmered with delight, spreading happiness and friendship.

Deep in the magical river, they encountered a family of fish struggling against the current. Zara and her friends created a safe path for them, guiding the fish to calmer waters. The crystal beamed with pride, spreading compassion and unity

In a hidden grove, they discovered a shy fawn feeling lost and scared. Zara gently approached, offering her hand. The fawn took a leap of faith, and their friendship bloomed. The crystal glowed with tenderness, spreading empathy and understanding.

Through dense thickets, they reached a clearing where a lonely tree stood. Zara and her friends decorated the tree with colourful ribbons and messages of kindness. The crystal gleamed with love, spreading warmth and acceptance.

As they journeyed deeper into the forest, they encountered a timid butterfly with tattered wings. Zara and her friends cared for the butterfly, mending its wings and watching it take flight. The crystal shimmered with compassion, spreading healing and renewal.

In a hidden cave, they stumbled upon a lost fox cub. Zara and her friends created a path of stones, guiding the cub back to its family. The crystal glowed with gratitude, spreading helpfulness and unity.

Along their path, they encountered a magical fountain guarded by a mischievous sprite. Zara and her friends shared a laugh with the sprite, embracing its playful tricks. The crystal sparkled with joy, spreading laughter and happiness.

As they reached the heart of the forest, they discovered a majestic tree with branches reaching for the sky. Zara and her friends planted seeds of kindness around the tree, nurturing it with love. The crystal radiated with harmony, spreading kindness and growth.

The enchanted forest came alive with the power of the kindness crystal. Mystical Animals of all kinds gathered,

basking in the warmth of their shared acts of kindness. Zara and her friends smiled, knowing they had made a difference.

News of the kindness crystal spread throughout the land, inspiring others to join the quest for kindness. The crystal's magic touched every corner of the forest, creating a tapestry of love and compassion.

Zara and her friends celebrated their successful journey, dancing and laughing under the starry night sky. The crystal glowed brilliantly, a beacon of hope and friendship for all who encountered it.

With hearts full of gratitude, Zara, her friends, and the other curious people bid farewell to the enchanted forest. They carried the lessons of kindness with them, vowing to continue spreading love wherever they went. The End.

Now that you have completed the
adventure with Zara and her
friends, can you help bring colour
to these pictures? Grab your
colouring pens and pencils!

ABOUT THE AUTHOR

I AM IAN, A JOYFUL AUTHOR ON A MISSION TO BRING SMILES AND LAUGHTER TO CHILDREN'S LIVES. WITH A PLAYFUL SPIRIT AND A PASSION FOR STORYTELLING, I CREATE ENCHANTING TALES THAT ENTERTAIN AND INSPIRE YOUNG READERS. THROUGH MY IMAGINATIVE NARRATIVES, I WEAVE IMPORTANT LIFE LESSONS INTO DELIGHTFUL ADVENTURES, FOSTERING BOTH IMAGINATION AND CHARACTER DEVELOPMENT. JOIN ME ON A JOURNEY OF LAUGHTER AND LEARNING AS WE EXPLORE THE MAGICAL WORLDS WITHIN THE PAGES OF MY BOOKS. TOGETHER, LET US CREATE CHERISHED MEMORIES AND IGNITE A LOVE FOR READING IN THE HEARTS OF CHILDREN EVERYWHERE.

Printed in Great Britain
by Amazon

23795093R00016